Y0-BUW-573

Easy-to-Do Book

MAKE-A-SWEET COOKBOOK

Written by Barbara Zeitz
Illustrated by Stan Tusan

Published by
READER'S DIGEST SERVICES, INC.
Pleasantville, New York

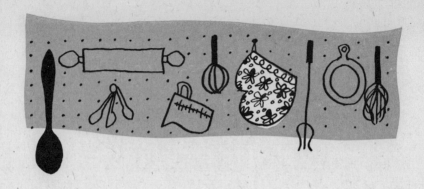

Introduction

This is a book giving you recipes for sweets which we usually think of as candies, cakes, cookies and ice cream. We have tried to use the most nutritious ingredients wherever possible, since most children love more sweets than their doctors, dentists and mothers would like them to have.

A good diet is necessary for a healthy and attractive body. Because children prefer an unlimited number of sweets to the foods that are best for them, mothers find it necessary to limit sweets and suggest a piece of fruit instead. However, when sweet treats are in order for dessert or an occasional snack, select one from these delicious recipes. All are easy to make and you'll find many old favorites, such as fudge, as well as many new and original recipes which will become favorites.

One last word, though, be sure to brush your teeth (whenever you can) after eating sweets. Let's call that the last step to each recipe. (Mom and your dentist would second this suggestion.)

Copyright © 1969 by Grosset & Dunlap, Inc. This edition is published by Reader's Digest Services, Inc. by arrangement with Grosset & Dunlap, Inc.

1st printing..January 1974

Printed in the U.S.A.

CONTENTS

SAFETY RULES

1. Be sure to have a grownup's permission before you start to cook. For safety's sake always have a grownup nearby while you are cooking.

2. Wash your hands and the table where you are going to work. Cleanliness is very important.

3. Have an adult light the oven and the burners on the range for you. When you are cutting or chopping with a knife, have a grownup show you how to do it first. No accidents, please!

4. Keep pot holders on hand to remove hot pans from the oven and the range. Never take the chance of burning yourself.

5. Turn handles of pots so they don't stick out beyond the range. This is so you don't bump against a pot and spill hot food on yourself.

6. Cleaning up after you have finished is important, too. Everything should be washed and put away.

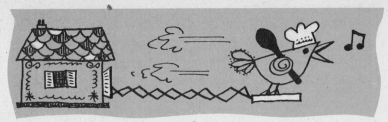

Before You Begin...

Now that you've decided to turn your talents to cooking, let's discuss a few of the do's and the importance of being careful. The kitchen is not a dangerous place if you know how to handle the utensils and appliances in it. But, if you are not aware of the accidents that can happen from carelessness, you, or someone working with you, could be seriously injured.

Be sure a grownup is in the house while you are cooking. Ask permission before starting to cook. It might be a good idea to read over the recipe with an adult so that you understand the steps thoroughly and so that you have all the ingredients in front of you. If you are a beginning cook, have someone who knows how, light the oven or burners on the range for you.

Your work area and your hands should be very clean. Leave the kitchen clean so that dinner, or the next meal can be started without having to mop up a glorious mess left by you. You want to be welcome in the kitchen next time.

Handle pots and pans that have been in the oven or on the range with pot holders. Turn pot handles so that they do not stick out, causing you to spill hot food on yourself.

Especially while you are learning your way around the kitchen, take your time and work carefully. You will be assured of good results and have a great deal of fun mixing, stirring and tasting. The kitchen is very much like a chemistry laboratory except that you can eat the results that come from the kitchen!

5

Today's supermarket is a wonderland of frozen, canned and packaged foods. In the beverage department you will find cans of frozen concentrated juices, large and small cans of juice on the shelves, or powdered concentrates you mix with water. Iced tea comes packaged in paper envelopes or in jars. You simply add water and in seconds you have a big, refreshing pitcherful. Homemade iced tea takes a lot longer and is much more complicated to make.

A suggestion for either parties or one or two servings of beverages is to combine frozen juices with carbonated soda and/or canned juice. Try orange and pineapple, lemonade and grape soda, cola and milk and floating marshmallow—combinations are unlimited. Experiment, with Mom's permission of course.

BLACK BEAUTY

2 small or 1 large jar
  strained prunes (Baby
  Food section of store)

⅔ cup orange juice
2 cups milk
1 pint vanilla ice cream

1. Chill first three ingredients.
2. With mixer or blender, blend all ingredients well.
   Pour the thick Black Beauties into four large
   glasses and serve.

7

LEMON FROTHY SHAKE

2 eggs
½ cup ice water
6 tablespoons lemon juice

½ cup sugar
2 cups cold milk
1 pint lemon sherbet

1. Beat the eggs with mixer.
2. Add cold water, lemon juice and sugar.
3. Pour milk into large bowl.
4. Add egg mixture to milk, beating constantly. Place scoops of lemon sherbet into four large glasses and pour the lemon shake over the top.

8

COLA QUICKIES

2 tablespoons sweet cream   Cola or root beer
1 large scoop chocolate
  ice cream

For each serving:

1. Place ice cream in tall glass.
2. Pour cream over ice cream.
3. Fill glass slowly with cola or root beer.

ROBINSON CRUSOE COOLER

2 cups fruit cocktail,   2 cups orange juice
  drained   Crushed ice
2 cups pineapple juice

1. Mash fruit cocktail with a fork in a bowl.
2. Divide among four tall glasses.
3. Add ½ cup of pineapple and ½ cup of orange juice to each glass.

Add a little crushed ice to each glass, stir and serve.

POLAR BEARS
(Orange Freeze)
Makes 4 servings

1 pint vanilla ice cream
½ of a 6-ounce can
concentrated frozen
orange juice

1. Let ice cream and concentrated orange juice thaw slightly.
2. Mix thoroughly with mixer or blender.

Divide evenly between four dessert dishes and place in the refrigerator until serving time.

SLUSH

Neopolitan Ice Cream (Vanilla, Chocolate and Strawberry) frozen hard, root beer, ice-cold

1. From the three-flavored ice cream, scoop off small spoonfuls and pile loosely in a drinking glass (don't pack the ice cream down).
2. Slowly pour the root beer in the glass.
   With a spoon, stir the mixture around a little and let stand for a minute.

When you eat the slush you'll find that the root beer has frozen around little particles of ice cream. It makes a nice thick "slushy" refresher, thick enough to eat with a spoon.

The cookie recipes are the favorites of most American children — Brownies, Old-Fashioned Sugar Cookies, Gingerbread Men, and other chocolate, peanut butter and fruit cookies. There are cookie mixes on the market and cookie rolls in the grocer's dairy department that you just slice and bake. Try these, if you like, but some rainy afternoon when you can't think of anything to do, try making cookies from scratch, using these recipes. You'll be proud of the fact that you made them yourself, and delighted with the praise you're going to receive from everyone who tastes one of your homebakes.

SIMPLE SIMON BROWNIES
(Very easy to make)

⅔ cup sifted flour   2 eggs
Pinch of salt   1 cup sugar
½ teaspoon baking powder   ½ cup chopped walnuts
2 squares baking chocolate 1 teaspoon vanilla
⅓ cup butter

1. Sift together flour, salt and baking powder.
2. In a double boiler, over hot water, melt chocolate squares and butter.
3. In a large bowl beat the eggs well.
4. Add sugar gradually.
5. Beat in the chocolate mixture.
6. Add flour mixture, nuts and vanilla.
7. Pour the brownie batter into a greased 8-inch square cake pan. Bake at 350° for 25 minutes. Cool in the pan and cut into squares.

13

BIG BABOONS
(Date-Orange Cookies you can't stop eating)
Makes about 36

1¼ cups (8 oz. package) dates, chopped
½ cup brown sugar (pack firmly)
½ cup butter
½ cup orange juice
1 teaspoon grated orange rind

2 eggs
1¼ cups sifted flour
1 teaspoon salt
¾ teaspoon baking soda
1 cup (6 oz. package) butterscotch morsels
1 cup chopped nuts

1. Over low heat, cook dates, brown sugar, butter, orange juice and orange rind, stirring constantly, until it begins to thicken.
2. Set aside and wait until it is cool.
3. Beat eggs in a small bowl and stir into mixture thoroughly.
4. Sift together flour, salt, baking soda.
5. Add to mixture in fourths, blending after each addition.
6. Stir in the butterscotch morsels and nuts.
7. Onto an ungreased cookie sheet, drop the dough by tablespoonfuls about 2 inches apart.
8. Bake at 375° for 10 minutes.
Remove to cooling rack.

14

CHOCOLATE NUT CHEWS
Makes 3 dozen

1 ½ cups sugar
¼ cup cocoa
½ cup evaporated milk
⅓ cup butter or
  margarine

⅓ cup peanut butter
1 teaspoon vanilla extract
1 ½ cups uncooked quick
  rolled oats
½ cup salted peanuts

1. In a large saucepan, mix together first four ingredients.
2. Cook until mixture boils, stirring constantly (two minutes).
3. Remove from heat.
4. Stir in the peanut butter until melted.
5. Now stir in vanilla, rolled oats and peanuts.
6. Using two teaspoons, drop on wax paper and let stand until solid.

PEANUT CHEWY CRISPS
About 36 cookies

1 cup peanut butter
1 cup sugar

½ cup undiluted
evaporated milk
4 teaspoons corn starch

1. Blend all ingredients in mixing bowl.
2. Drop by teaspoonfuls on ungreased cookie sheet.
3. Flatten each cookie with a fork dipped in water.
4. Bake in 350° oven for about 15 minutes.
   Cool 1 to 2 minutes and remove from cookie sheet.

PILGRIM'S PROGRESS

2 cups graham cracker
crumbs
1⅓ cups prepared
mince meat

1⅓ cups sweetened
condensed milk

1. Generously butter a 13 x 9 inch pan.
2. Pre-heat oven to 350°.
3. Thoroughly mix ingredients and place in pan.
4. Bake for 30 minutes.
   Cool in pan before cutting into squares.

OATMEAL OLD HATS
About 30 cookies

*3¼ cups quick-cooking
    oat cereal*
*¾ cup butter or margarine
    (do not use shortening)*

¾ cup sugar
1 teaspoon vanilla

1. In a large bowl mix together all ingredients.
2. Using your hands blend thoroughly, until dough becomes one lump.
3. With your fingers, take enough dough to form a ball 1 inch in diameter, and place on an ungreased cookie sheet.
4. Flatten with a fork. (If the dough sticks to the fork, dip it in a little water.)
5. Bake 15 to 20 minutes in a 350° oven. (Cookies will be lightly browned.)
   Before removing from cookie sheet, let cool for a few minutes.

17

COOKIES IN A WINK!

In the grocery store, you can find cookie mixes. To these you just add the liquids as the package directs, then bake.

There are also, in the frozen foods or dairy section of the store, packages of cookie dough already prepared. All you have to do to these is slice them and bake. This is the easy way, no doubt, but they are very good and the aroma of baking cookies will fill your house.

18

Make yourself your favorite candy—white fudge, chocolate fudge, peanut brittle, taffy, brown sugar candy, marshmallow and rice cereal candy, or chocolate spiders. Or make all of them and fill up a large clear glass candy dish to have on hand for TV nibblers, or to pass proudly when company drops in.

Almost everyone loves a piece of taffy, so for a gift occasion make up a batch or two of the taffy in different flavors and colors (as described in the recipe). Wrap the pieces of taffy individually, place them in a gift box, finish with colorful paper and a big ribbon bow.

Make the candy last a long time though, don't eat it all at once. Remember your teeth and how important it is to limit sweets.

19

SNOW WHITE'S FUDGE

1 package white frosting mix *½ cup chopped, candied cherries (red or green, or both) or white raisins*
2 tablespoons butter
3 tablespoons water

1. Butter a 9 x 5 x 3-inch pan.
2. In top of double boiler heat water and butter until butter is melted.
3. Add the package of frosting mix, stirring until smooth.
4. Heat an additional five minutes, stirring now and then.
5. Add cherries.
6. Pour into pan and let stand until solid; then cut into squares.

SEVEN DWARFS' NUT FUDGE

1⅔ cups sugar
2 tablespoons butter
½ teaspoon salt
⅔ cup evaporated milk
1½ cups semi-sweet
   chocolate morsels

¼ pound miniature
   marshmallows
½ cup chopped walnuts
1 teaspoon vanilla

1. Place sugar, butter, salt and evaporated milk in a large saucepan.

2. Stir until mixed and heat to a boil.

3. Boil gently for about five minutes, stirring all the while.

4. Turn off the heat and add the chocolate morsels, marshmallows, nuts and vanilla.

5. With a large spoon beat the candy mixture until chocolate and marshmallows are melted.

6. Grease an 8-inch square pan and pour in the fudge. Let it set until solid; then cut into squares.

SOUTHERN PEANUT BRITTLE

1 cup sugar
½ cup dark corn syrup
1 teaspoon butter
½ cup water

1 cup salted peanuts
(Spanish variety)
½ teaspoon vanilla
1 teaspoon baking soda

1. In a saucepan combine the sugar, dark corn syrup, butter and water.

2. Cook over moderate heat until, when a little is dropped from a spoon into a glass of cold water, it forms a soft ball.

3. Stir in peanuts.

4. Cook again until the candy mixture turns light brown in color.

5. Turn off the heat.

6. Mix in the baking soda and vanilla.

7. Grease a cookie sheet and pour the peanut brittle onto it.

8. Wet a large spoon with cold water and spread the candy over the entire cookie sheet, or so that it is no more than about ¼ inch thick. Let it cool and break into pieces when hard.

Peanut Brittle makes a nice gift for candy lovers, as well as taffy on the next page.

OLD FASHIONED TAFFY

2 cups sugar
1 cup water
½ cup vinegar
1 tablespoon butter

1 teaspoon vanilla
Pinch baking soda
Food coloring
Various flavoring extracts

1. In a saucepan stir until dissolved, sugar water and vinegar.
2. Cook over moderately low heat until, when dropped from a spoon into cold water, the mixture forms threads.
3. Now mix in the other ingredients.
4. Grease a cookie sheet and pour the taffy out to cool.
5. Butter your fingers and, when taffy is cool enough to handle, make several balls.
6. With your fingers, pull the taffy until it is satiny smooth.
7. Roll into a rope shape and cut into bite-sized pieces. Or, roll into tiny bite-sized balls. Wrap individually in clear cellophane or plastic wrap.

For taffy other than white and vanilla, add colorings and flavorings along with the last ingredients, before pouring out on the cookie sheet to cool. Store the wrapped taffy in a closed container.

Caution: When using flavorings or food colors, use very little at a time. A drop or two of each will do for a whole batch of taffy. Put a few drops in, stir thoroughly and taste. Then if more is needed, add another drop. Better have your taffy a little pale or under-flavored rather than too strong.

23

NOISY NIBBLERS

5 cups crisp rice cereal
40 marshmallows or 4 cups
   miniature marshmallows

¼ cup butter or
   margarine

1. Butter a 13 x 9-inch pan.
2. Melt butter in a large saucepan.
3. Add the marshmallows and heat over a very low flame, stirring constantly.
4. When marshmallows are melted and the mixture is syrupy, remove from the heat.
5. Add the rice cereal and stir so that the syrup and cereal are well mixed.
6. While still warm, place the mixture in the buttered pan and press down with a fork to fill the pan evenly.

   Let the mixture cool, then cut into squares.

DELECTABLE SPIDERS

1 pound sweet chocolate bar   *1 small can salted*
1 bag popped corn   *Virginia peanuts*

1. In the top of a large double boiler, over hot water, stir chocolate until completely melted.

2. Dump in the peanuts and popcorn and stir until well mixed.

3. Spread a piece of wax paper on a cookie sheet.

4. Drop small teaspoonfuls of the candy onto the paper and let harden.
   Remove to a plate when candy is set.
   Keep in a cool place.

OLD FASHIONED
BROWN SUGAR CANDY

About two dozen candies

2 cups brown sugar	*½ cup water*
3 teaspoons vinegar	*1 cup chopped mixed nuts*
3 teaspoons butter	*(pecans or walnuts)*

1. In a saucepan place brown sugar, vinegar, butter and water.

2. Stirring constantly, cook over low heat for about fifteen minutes.

3. The mixture is ready when it forms a thread, when dropped from a spoon into a glass of cold water.

4. Now stir in the nuts.

5. Turn off the heat and blend with a hand mixer or rotary beater until the candy is creamy.

6. On a flat surface, such as a cookie sheet, spread a piece of wax paper. Drop small teaspoonfuls onto the wax paper and let the candy cool.

DESSERTS

Easy to make, the perfect end to a good meal, these desserts will win you the compliments of your family and dinner guests. By making the dessert you take part of the chore of cooking off mother's hands. She'll be grateful and pleased to eat a dish she didn't have to prepare.

APRICOT DESSERT
About 6 servings

One no. 2½ can apricot halves
½ cup brown sugar
½ cup flour
¼ teaspoon salt
¼ teaspoon cinnamon
¼ cup butter

1. Grease a 9-inch pie plate.
2. Arrange apricot halves in bottom of pie plate, round sides up.
3. In a bowl mix together the brown sugar, flour, salt and cinnamon.
4. With a fork, blend in the butter until the mixture is crumbly.
5. Sprinkle over the apricots.
6. Bake in a 425° oven for 15 or 20 minutes. Crumbs will be golden brown.
   Serve warm, plain or with ice cream.

HEIDI'S ALPINE SNOW

1 3-oz. package straw-
berry gelatin (or any
favorite flavor)
1 cup boiling water

1 pint vanilla ice cream
4 vanilla wafers (flat,
thin cookies)

1. Boil the water and stir into gelatin until it is dissolved.

2. Stir in the ice cream until it is melted.

3. Place in the refrigerator for about five minutes, until the dessert begins to thicken.

4. On wax paper, on a flat surface, crush the vanilla wafers with a rolling pin, until they are crumbs.

5. Stir into your mixture.

   Spoon out into four dessert dishes and return to the refrigerator until thickened (fifteen minutes or so).

   Serve with two vanilla wafers alongside each dish.

APPLE CRISPIE
Makes about 6 servings

¼ cup butter
1 cup brown sugar
¼ cup flour
¾ cup rolled oats
Pinch of salt

1 teaspoon cinnamon
2 cups apple sauce
Frozen prepared whipped
cream

1. With a hand mixer or rotary beater blend butter and brown sugar until creamy.

2. Add the flour, rolled oats, salt and cinnamon.

3. Grease an 8-inch square baking dish and pour in the apple sauce.

4. Sprinkle the mixture over the top and press down lightly with a fork.

5. Bake in a 350° oven for 20 minutes.

To serve cut into squares and top each serving with a blob of whipped cream.

TUTTI-FRUITI IGLOO

6 generous servings

*1 quart ice cream
(vanilla, strawberry,
peach)
1 medium can fruit
cocktail, drained*

*1 pint container prepared
whipped cream
2 tablespoons chopped
walnuts*

Use a fancy 1½ quart ring mold.

1. Let the ice cream stand out of the refrigerator until soft.

2. In a bowl mix the ice cream and drained fruit cocktail.

3. Spoon into the ring mold and freeze for several hours until hard.

4. When ready to serve, dump the molded dessert onto a large plate and fill the hole with the whipped cream.

5. Sprinkle nuts on top of the whipped cream in the center.

   To serve, slice wedge-shaped pieces and place on a dessert plate. Spoon on top a little of the whipped cream and nuts.

   Thin, crisp cookies on the side are nice with this dessert.

30

ORANGE MARSHMALLOW
JUNGLE TREAT
Enough to serve 6

30 marshmallows
1 cup orange juice

*Frozen prepared whipped
cream, 1 pint container*

1. Heat orange juice to boiling point.
2. Cut up marshmallows into small pieces and place in a bowl.
3. Pour hot orange juice over the marshmallows and let the mixture stand until the marshmallows are soft and the mixture is cool.
4. Place in the refrigerator to set.
5. Mix the whipped cream with the orange marshmallow and place in the refrigerator for several hours.

FRUIT DESSERT BOWL

4 generous servings

Use all fresh fruits whenever possible. Otherwise use a canned variety.

2 peaches

1 cup blueberries

1 cup strawberries

1 cantaloupe melon

½ cup orange juice

½ cup coconut

Wash the fruit before you begin.

1. Cut up peaches and melon into bite-sized pieces.
2. Place these along with the blueberries and strawberries in a bowl.
3. Pour orange juice over the fruit and place in the refrigerator for several hours.
4. When ready to serve, add the coconut and toss lightly.

Serve in dessert dishes.

ORANGE-PINEAPPLE DEELISH!!

1 medium can mandarin oranges

1 medium can pineapple tidbits

⅓ package miniature marshmallows

½ can shredded coconut

1 pint sour cream

1. Drain well, orange sections and pineapple tidbits.
2. In a large bowl combine all ingredients and refrigerate until serving time.

   Do not prepare this dessert any more than two hours before serving.

CHERRY DESSERT AND SAUCE
Serves 4

Cake:

2 cups canned baking
    cherries (sour)
½ cup chopped walnuts
1¼ cups sugar
1 cup flour
½ teaspoon cinnamon
1 tablespoon baking soda
Pinch of salt
1 egg
1 tablespoon melted butter

Sauce:

Cherry juice (saved)
1 tablespoon cornstarch
½ cup sugar
½ teaspoon salt
1 tablespoon butter

To make cake:

1. Drain cherries and save the juice.
2. In a large bowl combine nuts and cherries.
3. Add the dry ingredients: sugar, flour, cinnamon soda and salt.
4. Beat the egg lightly with a fork and pour into the mixture.
5. Melt butter over very low flame and add, stirring well with a fork.
6. Lightly grease an 8-inch square cake pan and pour the mixture onto it.
7. Bake at 350° for 45 minutes.

To make sauce:

1. To cherry juice add enough water to make 1 cup liquid.
2. Combine ingredients in a saucepan and cook over low heat until sauce is thickened.

When cake is done, serve warm topped with ice cream and sauce poured over ice cream.

BAKED APPLES

4 large red cooking-apples
½ teaspoon cinnamon
½ cup sugar

⅔ cup water
2 tablespoons sugar
A drop of red food
coloring

1. Wash the apples and with an apple coring utensil, scoop out the cores of the apples.
2. With a knife, pare off the apple skin about one quarter of the way down.
3. Place in an ovenproof shallow dish with the pared sides up.
4. Boil the sugar, food coloring, cinnamon and water for 10 minutes.
5. Pour over apples.
6. Bake in a 350° oven for about an hour. Baste frequently (open oven door and with a spoon pour the syrup over the top of the apples several times during the baking).
7. When apples are tender (test by sticking them with a sharp knife), remove from oven.
8. Turn oven up to broil.
9. Sprinkle the 2 tablespoons of sugar over the top of the apples.
10. Place under the broiler for a few minutes to brown the apples and sugar.

Serve warm with whipped cream or ice cream on top.

36

PINEAPPLE WHIP

One no. 2 can crushed
  pineapple
1 package lemon gelatin

2 tablespoons sugar
1 cup heavy cream

1. In a sieve, drain the crushed pineapple, saving the juice.
2. Measure the syrup and add enough water to make 1½ cups liquid.
3. Pour this in a saucepan and bring to a boil.
4. Mix in a medium-sized bowl, sugar with gelatin mix and pour in the boiling liquid.
5. Stir until mixture is thoroughly dissolved.
6. Place in refrigerator until slightly thickened.
7. Whip the cream until firm.
8. Into the gelatin, fold the pineapple and whipped cream.
9. Spoon into six fancy sherbet glasses and place in the refrigerator until set.

Serve sherbet glass on a dessert plate and place a thin French cookie or vanilla wafer alongside.

BAKED CUSTARD
6 servings

4 eggs

¼ cup sugar

Pinch of salt

2 ¼ cups milk

1 teaspoon vanilla

Ground nutmeg

1. Preheat the oven at 300°.
2. Break eggs into a large bowl. Beat with a hand mixer until the eggs are fluffy.
3. Add sugar and salt. Beat until thick.
4. Add milk and vanilla and beat again until mixture is thoroughly blended.
5. Arrange custard cups next to each other and divide custard evenly among the six cups (Pour the mixture through a fine sieve).
6. Shake ground nutmeg on top of each.
7. Place custard cups in a baking pan about 2 inches high. Place on the oven rack.
8. Pour hot water into the pan being careful not to get any into the custard cups. Pour until water comes about three quarters of the way up the side of the custard cups.
9. Bake for about an hour. (Custard cups are done when an inserted knife comes out clean.)

Serve plain or with maple syrup on top.

ANNA-BANANA SHERBET

1 quart or 6 large servings

4 very ripe bananas *2 cups evaporated milk*
2 lemons *2 cups whole milk*
2 cups sugar

1. Mash the bananas with a fork.
2. Squeeze juice from lemons and strain to remove seeds.
3. Combine all ingredients in a bowl and mix well.
4. Pour into an empty ice cube tray and freeze.

VANILLA, CHOCOLATE AND BUTTERSCOTCH PUDDINGS

Vanilla, chocolate, butterscotch and some other flavored puddings are available in packages in the grocery store. Some puddings are to be cooked and some are instant (they need only mixing with a rotary beater). All you need are the pudding mix and two cups of milk; prepare according to package directions.

Pudding can be spooned into serving dishes and placed in the refrigerator to set. Or, use puddings as pie fillings. (See page 51 for pie recipes.)

You can vary pudding mixes to make your own creations. Make two packages of pudding and place in parfait glasses: first one flavor, then the other. Place a layer of miniature marshmallows in the middle and top with marshmallows.

On top of vanilla pudding, place a spoonful of strawberry preserves.

Top chocolate and butterscotch pudding with whipped cream.

SOME HOW-TO'S OF CAKE BAKING

Try your hand at making a cake for dessert or a party. There are no tricks to it, only the few basic steps required by most recipes.

Preparation: Preheat your oven as the recipe directs. Make sure the temperature is right. The success of your cake depends a great deal on this.

Most cake recipes require that you lightly grease and sprinkle flour on the pans. Watch the directions.

Steps:

1. Dry ingredients: Measure exactly. When the recipe calls for a cup of sifted flour, sift before you measure. Add dry ingredients and sift again.
2. Liquid ingredients: Usually, the shortening, sugar and liquid ingredients are blended together in another bowl. Dry ingredients are then added to the liquid. Some recipes vary, but most follow the above directions.
3. Is the cake done? After the recommended time for baking has elapsed, test by sticking a sharp knife into the middle of the cake. If it comes out "clean," that is, no sticky particles clinging to the knife, the cake is finished baking. If sticky particles do cling to the knife, return the cake to the oven for a few more minutes.
4. Cooling the cake properly: Let the cake remain in the pan for a few minutes after baking. Then, place a wire cake cooling rack on top of the cake pan. Turn upside down and let the cake cool until it is room temperature.

Frosting: Make the frosting according to the recipes on page 46. Place a layer on a serving plate and spread about ⅓ of the frosting on top. Place the second layer on top and use another third of the frosting to cover the sides of both layers. Use the remaining frosting for the top of the cake. Spread evenly. If the frosting does not spread easily, dip your knife into a little water.

Serving: To serve your cake, cut according to the diagrams on this page.

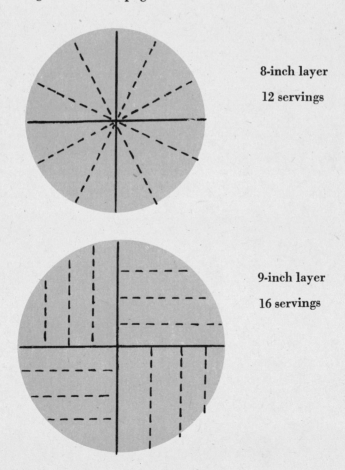

8-inch layer

12 servings

9-inch layer

16 servings

ORANGE CAKE

2 cups sifted flour
1 ¼ cups sugar
2 ½ teaspoons baking powder
1 teaspoon salt
⅓ cup soft butter or margarine

¾ cup milk
¼ cup orange juice
1 teaspoon grated orange rind
1 teaspoon vanilla
1 large egg or two small eggs

1. In a large bowl sift together flour, sugar, baking powder and salt.
2. Add shortening, milk and vanilla.
3. With a hand mixer on medium speed, beat for two minutes.
4. Add orange juice, egg and grated orange rind.
5. Beat another two minutes.
6. Grease and lightly dust with flour two 8-inch layer cake pans.
7. Divide batter in half and pour into pans.
8. Bake at 350° for 30 minutes.

Cool layers on wire rack.

Choose a frosting from the recipes on page 46.

POUNDCAKE

3 cups sifted flour
1½ teaspoons baking
    powder
Pinch salt
½ teaspoon nutmeg

1 cup soft butter
1½ cups sugar
1 teaspoon vanilla
3 eggs
½ cup milk

Lightly grease a 10 x 5 x 3-inch loaf pan.

Sift together *three* times, flour, baking powder, salt and nutmeg.

1. In a large bowl place butter, sugar and vanilla.
2. Blend thoroughly with a hand mixer.
3. Add eggs and beat on medium speed until very light and fluffy. This may take as long as **four** minutes.
4. At low speed on the mixer, alternately blend in milk and flour mixture until batter is smooth.
5. Pour into the loaf pan and bake for 1 hour and 10 minutes, or until a knife inserted in the middle comes out clean (nothing sticking to the knife).
6. Serve plain, dust with confectioners' sugar, or use a basic frosting recipe (see page 47).

You could toast slices of poundcake, add a scoop of ice cream and top with chocolate or fudge sauce.

43

GINGERBREAD

1 package gingerbread mix
1 medium-sized jar applesauce
1 pint frozen whipped cream

1. Prepare gingerbread as package directs. Keep in a warm place.
2. At serving time, cut into squares and top each with a spoonful of applesauce and a blob of whipped cream.

VERY EASY
CHOCOLATE CAKE

2 cups sifted flour
1¾ cups sugar
¾ cup cocoa
1¼ teaspoons baking soda
½ teaspoon baking powder
1 teaspoon salt

¾ cup vegetable
*   shortening or*
*   margarine*
¾ cup milk
1 teaspoon vanilla
½ cup milk
3 eggs

1. Grease and then line with wax paper two 9-inch layer cake pans.

2. Sift together the dry ingredients (first six ingredients) in a large bowl.

3. Add the shortening, ¾ cup milk and vanilla.

4. Beat at medium speed with the mixer for 2½ minutes.

5. Add the eggs and ½ cup milk and beat 2½ minutes longer. (You must beat the batter 5 minutes all together.)

6. Divide the batter evenly between the two layer cake pans.

7. Bake in a 350° oven for about 35 minutes.

8. Select a frosting from the recipes on page 46.

FROSTINGS

Floating Cloud Frosting:

> 1 ¼ cups white corn syrup
> 2 egg whites
> Pinch of salt
> 1 teaspoon vanilla

1. Heat the corn syrup in a saucepan until it boils.
2. At highest speed on hand mixer, beat egg whites until soft peaks form when you raise the beaters.
3. Add the salt.
4. While beating, slowly pour in the syrup. Frosting will become fluffy.
5. With a large spoon carefully fold in the vanilla.

Vanilla Cream Frosting:

2 cups heavy cream
1 cup confectioners' sugar
Pinch of salt

1. Chill a medium-sized bowl, and the beaters to your mixer.
2. Combine ingredients and beat until thick and creamy enough to spread.

Chocolate Cream Frosting:

Use above recipe, adding ½ cup cocoa to ingredients.

Butter Cream Frosting:

½ cup soft butter
3 cups sifted confectioners' sugar
Pinch salt
About ¼ cup milk
1½ teaspoons vanilla

1. In a medium bowl blend, at medium speed on mixer, butter, sugar and salt until light and fluffy.
2. Still beating, add remaining sugar and just enough of the milk to make it spread well.
3. Add vanilla and beat a few more seconds.

Orange Butter Cream Frosting:

To above recipe add 1 teaspoon grated orange rind and instead of ¼ cup milk, add 1 tablespoon orange juice and 1 tablespoon milk.

CAKE MIXES

The grocery store has many cake mixes on the shelves. They are almost as good as the cakes you prepare from scratch. You will find white cake, yellow cake, chocolate, devil's food, angel or sponge cake, and many more. Try any one and make your own frosting, or use a frosting mix. Yes! There are even frosting mixes. But our recipes for frosting are so easy, they are scarcely more trouble to prepare than a mix.

However, take advantage of any short-cuts available. If you are in the mood for a cake but just don't feel like doing the measuring of ingredients, use a cake mix. It will be almost as much fun to make as the "real thing", made from scratch.

PIES

The pie recipes given here are very easy to do. You will not have to roll out crusts, which is tricky even for experienced cooks, but you have only to press the pie "dough" against the sides of the pie plate. The fillings are so easy to prepare you'll be finished in no time!

Pie Crust:

> *18 graham crackers*
> *½ stick butter or margarine*
> *2 tablespoons sugar*

1. Melt butter or margarine in a small saucepan over the lowest possible heat on your range.
2. On a flat surface move a rolling pin over the graham crackers until they are fine crumbs.
3. In a mixing bowl combine with a fork the crumbs, butter and sugar.
4. In an 8- or 9-inch pie plate, press the mixture against the sides of the plate and the bottom.
5. Even out with your hands.
6. Bake for about 8 minutes in a 350° oven. Cool before filling.

Banana Cream Pie filling:

1 package vanilla pudding
2 bananas

1. Prepare pudding as package directs.
2. Slice thinly one banana and stir into the pudding.
3. Fill a baked pie shell with the pudding mixture.
4. Slice the other banana and arrange slices evenly on top of the pie.
5. Serve plain or top each slice with a spoonful of whipped cream.

Chocolate Cream Pie filling:

1 package chocolate pudding
1 pint frozen whipped cream

1. Prepare chocolate pudding and pour into baked pie shell.
2. Top pie with spoonfuls of whipped cream, or spread evenly on top.
3. Arrange chocolate bits in a circle on top of the whipped cream.

Use any of the pudding mixes to fill pie shells. Top with miniature marshmallows, whipped cream, or make up your own concoctions.

Strawberry Ice Cream Pie filling:

1 package strawberry gelatin
1 cup boiling water
1 pint frozen strawberries, thawed
1 pint vanilla ice cream

1. In a mixing bowl, stir together the gelatin and boiling water until the gelatin is dissolved.

2. Add the ice cream and stir until it is melted.

3. Mash the strawberries with a fork and add to the mixture. Place in the refrigerator for 5 minutes.

5. With a beater, blend the mixture until it becomes light and frothy.

6. Pour the pie filling into the baked pie shell.

7. Spread evenly and cover with plastic food wrap.

8. Chill in the refrigerator for several hours before serving.

SWEETS FROM FOREIGN LANDS

Almost every country in the world has its own food specialty. Here are some favorite sweets from foreign countries.

APPLE CAKE FROM NORWAY
Makes 4 desserts

2 slices whole wheat bread   *2 cups applesauce*
2 tablespoons butter   *Whipped cream*
2 tablespoons sugar

1. Let the bread slices become stale and crush to make bread crumbs.
2. In a frying pan melt butter.
3. Add the bread crumbs and stir with a fork until blended.
4. Add the sugar and stir the mixture gently until it becomes crispy.
5. Divide the crumb mixture among four dessert plates and pack down slightly with a fork.
6. Put a spoonful or two of applesauce on top of the crumb crust and add whipped cream.

RICE PUDDING FROM CENTRAL AMERICA

Makes 4 large servings

⅓ cup regular white rice
½ teaspoon salt
½ cup sugar

½ teaspoon nutmeg or
   allspice
½ cup raisins
1 quart milk

1. Butter an ovenproof 1½-quart baking dish.
2. Stir the dry ingredients in the baking dish and pour in milk.
3. Bake at 325° for three hours.
4. Stir the pudding three or four times during the first hour of baking to prevent the rice from settling to the bottom of the dish.

SPANISH FRUIT AND NUT SWEETS
Makes about 50 candies

1 cup pitted dates
½ cup raisins
½ cup candied cherries
1½ cups pecan nuts

1 cup almonds
1½ cups walnuts
Confectioners' sugar

1. Chop the fruit and nut ingredients in a food grinder.
2. Sprinkle table or work area with confectioners' sugar and knead ingredients until they are blended and smooth.
3. Roll small amounts of mixture in palms of your hands to form candy balls about ¾ inch in diameter.

55

FRENCH MOUSSE AU CHOCOLAT

(A light and delicious chocolate pudding, made
easy for beginning cooks)

½ cup semi-sweet chocolate morsels
3 eggs separated
1 teaspoon vanilla
Frozen container of whipped cream

1. Separate the eggs, yolks in one bowl, whites in another.
2. In the top of a double boiler, over hot water, melt chocolate morsels.
3. Remove the double boiler top and with a spoon beat in the egg yolks and vanilla.
4. With a hand mixer or rotary beater whip the egg whites until stiff peaks form.
5. With a spatula, very gently fold the egg whites into the chocolate.
6. Spoon into dessert dishes.
7. To serve, top with a little whipped cream.

56

Holidays and Special Occasions

Some of our foods are traditional, that is, they are usually served only on holidays and special occasions. The following recipes are for Thanksgiving, Christmas, or a birthday for someone special.

SWEET CRANBERRY MOLD
FOR THANKSGIVING

6 servings

2 cups fresh whole
cranberries
2 apples
1 cup sugar
1 package lemon gelatin
1 cup boiling water

½ cup pineapple juice
½ cup seeded grape
halves
¼ cup chopped walnuts
1½ quart ring mold

1. Wash the cranberries and apples in cold water.

2. Do not peel the apples, but cut them in quarters and cut out the core.

3. In a food chopper, using a medium blade, grind the apples and cranberries. Catch them in a large bowl.

4. Add sugar and stir well.

5. Dissolve gelatin in boiling water and add pineapple juice.

6. Chill in refrigerator until slightly thickened.

7. Mix together the gelatin, cranberries and apples, grapes and walnuts.

8. Rinse the mold with cold water and pour in the mixture.

9. Chill until firm.

About one-half hour before serving, place a serving plate in the refrigerator to chill. At dinnertime, place the plate over the mold and, holding plate to mold tightly, turn upside down. The cranberry mold will be right side up on the plate. You can decorate the cranberry mold with pineapple rings cut in half and placed artistically around the edge.

CHRISTMAS NUT BREAD —
THREE LOAVES

1½ cups sifted flour
1½ cups sugar
1 teaspoon baking powder
1 teaspoon salt
2 pounds pitted dates
1 eight-ounce bottle
  maraschino cherries

2 pounds shelled pecan
  nuts
1 pound shelled Brazil
  nuts
5 eggs
1 teaspoon vanilla

1. Sift together dry ingredients: flour, sugar, baking powder and salt.
2. Add fruit and nuts (whole, if you like, or chopped).
3. Beat eggs and vanilla.
4. Add flour mixture and stir well.
5. Grease and flour three loaf pans.
6. Divide dough evenly and bake for 1 hour in a 325° oven.
   Let cool to room temperature before slicing.

POPCORN, NUT, AND RAISIN
CHRISTMAS TREE

6 cups popped popcorn
1 cup raisins
1 cup tiny Spanish
  peanuts

⅓ cup light corn syrup
⅓ cup water
1 cup sugar

You will need: Toothpicks, 12-inch Styrofoam cone, a rope of Christmas green (not more than 1 inch in diameter).

1. Lightly butter a very large bowl.

2. Pour in popcorn, raisins and Spanish peanuts.

3. In a saucepan, place sugar, corn syrup and water.

4. Cook over medium-high flame until syrup reaches 240° on candy thermometer, or until a drop of the mixture forms a soft ball when dropped in a small bowl of ice water. Do not stir syrup.

5. Pour the syrup mixture over the popcorn, nuts and raisins.

6. Mix well with two large spoons or forks.

7. Allow the mixture to cool until it's comfortable to handle.

8. Butter your hands well and roll the candy dough into 1-inch balls.

9. Place on wax paper to harden.

10. Stick a toothpick in each ball with enough of the toothpick protruding so that it will be easy to stick the balls into the Styrofoam tree later.

11. Work quickly, rolling the balls, so that the candy mixture does not harden before you finish.

12. Wind the greens around the Styrofoam form and fasten with glue or pins.

13. When your popcorn balls are completely hardened, stick them in place by the toothpicks.

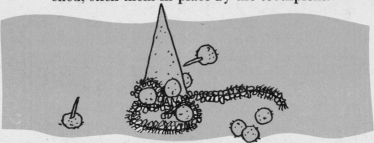

ICE CREAM BIRTHDAY CAKE

1 package devil's food cake mix
2 one-pint packages strawberry ice cream
Vanilla frosting recipe from page 47.

1. Prepare the cake mix as package directs, baking in two 9-inch layer pans.

2. Wrap in plastic food wrap and freeze for several hours.

3. Remove ice cream from freezer so that it becomes soft enough to spread.

4. When layer cake is frozen, spread ice cream on top of each layer and return to freezer.

5. Prepare frosting.

6. When ice cream is frozen hard on top of the layer cake, place one layer on top of the other and cover the top and sides of the cake with frosting.

7. Replace in the freezer until serving time.

You can place candle holders and candles on the cake and light them just before you carry it in to the table.

LOW-CALORIE SWEETS

If anyone in your family is on a diet—either to lose weight or cut down on the amount of sugar he eats— here are some recipes you can try so that the dieter can enjoy a sweet, too.

FRESH FRUIT GELATIN

1 package low-calorie gelatin (any flavor)
½ cup blueberries
½ cup diced cantaloupe
½ cup diced peaches

1. Prepare gelatin as package directs, by pouring 1 cup boiling water over gelatin.
2. Stir to dissolve.
3. Add 1 cup cold water.
4. Refrigerate until gelatin is set but not yet firm.
5. Stir in fruit and put back in refrigerator until firm.

You can make the dessert in one large bowl or in individual dessert dishes.

LOW-CALORIE EGG CREAM

⅓ cup powdered skim milk
Dietetic soda (any flavor)
Ice cubes

1. Fill a drinking glass with ice cubes.
2. Pour in soda until glass is about ¾ full.
3. Gradually add skim milk powder, stirring vigorously until all powder has been added.

FRESH FRUIT MALTED

1 cup skimmed milk
1 peach diced into small pieces
Few drops of artificial sweetener
3 ice cubes

1. Place all ingredients in blender and switch on for about 30 seconds, until the malted is frothy.

½ cup blueberries or strawberries or other fresh fruit may be substituted for the peach.

Glossary

Baking is cooking in the oven at a certain temperature. The recipe will tell you how hot the oven should be.

Basting is pouring the drippings from the pan onto whatever you are baking, as directed by the recipe.

Batter is the mixture of flower, milk, eggs and other ingredients that go into making your cake.

Beating is fast stirring with an egg beater, spoon or mixer, so the ingredients are smooth.

Blending is mixing so thoroughly that the ingredients become either a different color, taste differently or change thickness.

Boiling is cooking a liquid in a pot over high heat until bubbles rise and break on the surface.

Chopping is cutting food into small pieces with a knife.

Chilling is moderately cooling something in the refrigerator.

Draining is letting the liquid trickle off through a strainer or similar utensil.

Dusting is coating the whole surface so that it looks as if it were powdered.

Folding is to combine ingredients by gently moving a spoon over and through a mixture.

Grating is making little shreds by rubbing food on a "grater".

Greasing a pan is done by rubbing it with butter or vegetable shortening.

Paring is cutting away or trimming off the rind or skin that covers the fruit or vegetable.

Pinch is a very small amount—as much as you can squeeze between your finger and your thumb.

Separate eggs by gently cracking shells and holding yolk in one shell half while letting the white drip into a bowl; then drop the yolk in another bowl.

Sifting is putting flower through a sieve to make it lighter.

Sprinkle by scattering drops over the surface.

Thawing is melting something so that it becomes soupy or soft.

Tossing is gently lifting repeatedly, with a fork and spoon.

Whipping is beating into a froth with an egg beater or mixer.

Whip Cream in a chilled bowl with chilled beaters. When cream is soupy, add vanilla and sugar. Beat again until cream is slightly stiff.